T0378714

DINNER
Across Cultures
Recipes from Around the World

by
Chelsey Luciow

CAPSTONE PRESS
a capstone imprint

Dabble Lab is published by Capstone Press, an imprint of Capstone.
1710 Roe Crest Drive, North Mankato, Minnesota 56003
capstonepub.com

Library of Congress Cataloging-in-Publication Data is available on the Library of Congress website.
ISBN: 9781669093138 (hardcover)
ISBN: 9781669093091 (ebook PDF)

Summary: Get a taste of the world when you cook up dinner across cultures! From Hungarian goulash to Indonesian mie goreng to Argentinian empanadas, these easy-to-make recipes are sure to make your evening bright.

Image Credits: Adobe Stock: donatas1205 (background), 15, 28, FomaA, 12 (butter), Sharmin, 12 (background); Mighty Media, Inc. (project photos)
Design Elements: Adobe Stock: byMechul, zhaluldesign; Mighty Media, Inc.

Editorial Credits
Editor: Jessica Rusick
Designer: Denise Hamernik

Printed and bound in Malaysia. 6096

Table of Contents

Cooking Up Dinner 4

Hungarian Goulash 6

Spanish Tuna Pasta 9

Indonesian Mie Goreng. 10

Ukrainian Borscht 13

Norwegian Pytt i Panna Hash 14

Mexican Lentil Soup 17

Cuban Beans and Rice 18

Taiwanese Three-Cup Chicken 21

Sierra Leonean Groundnut Soup . . . 22

Argentinean Empanadas 25

Polish Haluski 26

Senegalese Chicken Yassa 29

English Cottage Pie 30

Read More. 32

Internet Sites 32

About the Author 32

Cooking Up
DINNER

In many cultures, dinner is a time to eat together with family and relax after a long day. Kids in countries around the world eat all kinds of dinners. Many meals are beloved dishes in the cultures they come from. Make Senegalese chicken, Spanish tuna pasta, Ukrainian borscht, and more to experience foods from many cultures!

Basic Supplies

- frying pan
- grater
- juicer
- knife and cutting board
- measuring cups and spoons
- mixing bowls
- parchment paper
- rolling pin
- spatula
- whisk

Kitchen Tips

1. Ask an adult for permission before you make a recipe.

2. Ask an adult for help when using a knife, blender, grater, stove, or oven. Wear oven mitts when removing items from the oven or microwave.

3. Read through the recipe and set out all ingredients and supplies before you start working.

4. Using metric tools? Use the conversion chart on the right to make your recipe measure up.

5. Wash your hands before and after you handle food. Wash and dry fresh produce before use.

6. When you are done making food, clean your work surface and wash dirty dishes. Put all supplies and ingredients back where you found them.

Standard	Metric
¼ teaspoon	1.25 grams or milliliters
½ teaspoon	2.5 g or mL
1 teaspoon	5 g or mL
1 tablespoon	15 g or mL
¼ cup	57 g (dry) or 60 mL (liquid)
⅓ cup	75 g (dry) or 80 mL (liquid)
½ cup	114 g (dry) or 125 mL (liquid)
⅔ cup	150 g (dry) or 160 mL (liquid)
¾ cup	170 g (dry) or 175 mL (liquid)
1 cup	227 g (dry) or 240 mL (liquid)
1 quart	950 mL

Hungarian Goulash

Goulash (GOO-lahsh) was first cooked by Hungarian herdsmen hundreds of years ago. The dish gets its color and flavor from paprika, Hungary's national spice.

Ingredients
(makes 4 servings)

- 3 tablespoons butter
- 1 large onion, chopped
- 1 pound beef stew meat, cubed
- 3 cloves garlic, minced
- 3 tablespoons paprika
- 1 teaspoon salt
- ½ teaspoon pepper
- 2 cups beef broth
- 15-ounce can diced tomatoes
- 2 carrots, diced
- 2 large potatoes, cut into small cubes

1. Melt the butter in a pot over medium-high heat. Add the onion and cook until just browned, about 15 minutes.

2. Add the meat to the pot and cook it until it browns, about 8 to 10 minutes. Add the garlic and cook for another minute.

3. Remove the pot from the heat. Add the paprika, salt, and pepper and stir to coat the meat mixture. Add the beef broth and tomatoes. Return the pot to the stovetop and bring it to a boil over high heat. Then reduce the heat to low, cover the pot, and simmer the goulash for 30 minutes.

4. Add the carrots and potatoes to the pot and increase the heat to medium. Cook the goulash until the carrots, potatoes, and meat are soft and cooked through, about 30 to 40 minutes. Add more salt and pepper to taste.

Herdsman's Meat

The word *goulash* comes from the Hungarian term *gulyás hús* (GOOL-yash hoos), which means "herdsman's meat."

Food Words

"Tuna" in Spanish is *atún* (ah-TOON), "olive" is *aceituna* (ah-say-TOO-nah), and "tomato" is *tomate* (toh-MAH-tay).

Spanish Tuna Pasta

Tuna is common in Spain's coastal regions. This dish is popular with students because it is quick and easy to make.

Ingredients
(makes 6 servings)

- 12 ounces dry pasta (fusilli, rotini, or gemelli work well)
- 3 tablespoons olive oil
- ½ medium onion, diced
- 3 cloves garlic, minced
- 14-ounce can crushed tomatoes
- 10-ounce can tuna, drained
- 10 large green olives, pitted and sliced
- salt and pepper to taste
- ½ cup manchego or mozzarella cheese, grated

1. Cook and drain the noodles according to the package's directions. The noodles should be tender but still a bit firm and chewy. Set them aside.

2. Heat the olive oil in a large frying pawn. Add the onion and cook until soft, about 5 minutes. Add the garlic and cook the mixture for another 1 minute.

3. Stir in the tomatoes and tuna. Cook the mixture on medium-high heat for 5 minutes.

4. Stir in the sliced olives and salt and pepper.

5. Add the drained pasta and stir well to coat the noodles in the sauce. Top each serving with grated cheese.

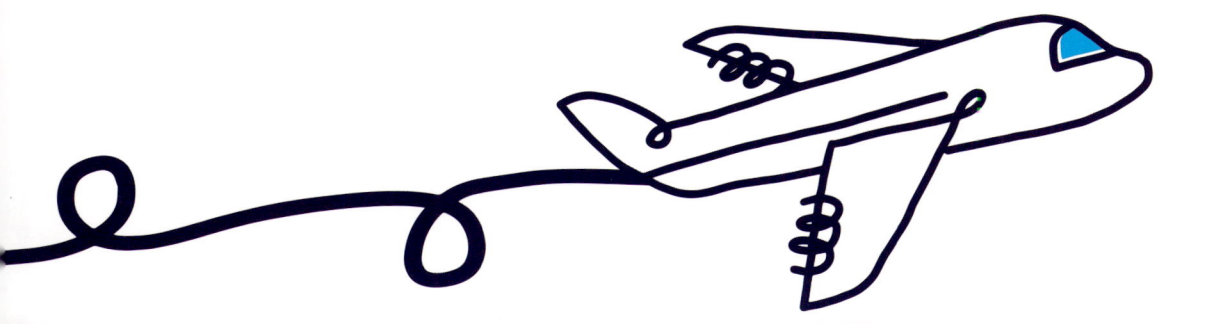

Indonesian
Mie Goreng

This fried noodle dish is a popular Indonesian street food. Its sweet flavor comes from kecap manis (KAY-kap MAH-nees), an Indonesian soy sauce.

Ingredients
(makes 4 servings)

- 2 tablespoons kecap manis (or 1 tablespoon soy sauce and 1 tablespoon honey)
- 4 teaspoons soy sauce
- 1 tablespoon oyster sauce
- 2 tablespoons ketchup
- 1 teaspoon sriracha
- 2 teaspoons sesame oil
- 3 instant noodle packets
- 2 tablespoons vegetable oil
- 2 eggs, whisked
- 3 cloves garlic, minced
- 4 ounces boneless, skinless chicken, cut into bite-size pieces
- 2 cups finely sliced green cabbage
- 1 cup bean sprouts, fresh or canned
- 3 green onions, chopped

1. Mix the kecap manis, soy sauce, oyster sauce, ketchup, sriracha, and sesame oil in a bowl. This is the sauce. (To substitute kecap manis, mix 1 tablespoon soy sauce and honey in a microwave-safe bowl. Heat the mixture in 10-second bursts, stirring between each one, until the honey is dissolved.)

2. Cook the noodles according to the packages' directions. Do not use the spice packets.

3. Heat 1 tablespoon vegetable oil in a large pan. Add the eggs and cook for 1 minute. Then flip, stir, or cut the eggs into small pieces. Remove them from the pan.

4. Add the remaining oil, garlic, and chicken to the pan. Cook for about 5 minutes, or until the chicken starts turning white.

5. Stir in the cabbage and bean sprouts. Cover and allow the cabbage to wilt for 2 minutes.

6. Add the cooked noodles, green onion, and sauce to the pan. Stir for 2 minutes to warm the sauce and coat the noodles.

7. Stir the cooked egg pieces into the mixture. Serve in bowls with chopsticks!

Fried Noodles

Mie goreng (MEE goh-rheng) means "fried noodles" in Indonesian. The dish was likely introduced to Indonesia by Chinese immigrants.

Bread and Butter

Borscht is commonly served with bread and butter, or *khlib z maslom* (HLEEB iz MAZ-luhm).

Ukrainian Borscht

Borscht (BOHRSHT), or beet soup, is the national dish of Ukraine. Historians believe Ukrainians first made borscht as early as the 400s!

Ingredients
(makes 6 servings)

- 2 large beets, peeled
- 1 tablespoon butter
- 1 cup diced onion
- 1 cup diced celery
- 1 cup chopped cabbage
- 2 cloves garlic, minced
- 8 cups beef, vegetable, or chicken broth
- 14-ounce can diced tomatoes
- 2 medium carrots, peeled and grated
- 1 large potato, peeled and diced
- ½ cup fresh dill weed, plus extra
- salt and pepper to taste
- sour cream (optional)
- rye bread (optional)
- butter (optional)

1. Dice one beet. Grate the other beet into a small bowl. Set the beets aside.

2. Melt the butter in a pot over medium-high heat. Add the onion, celery, and cabbage. Cook the vegetables until they soften, about 5 minutes.

3. Add the garlic, broth, and tomatoes to the pot. Bring the borscht to a boil. Then lower the heat to medium.

4. Add the beets, carrots, and potatoes to the pot.

5. Simmer the borscht over medium heat until the beets and potatoes are soft, about 15 minutes. A fork should be able to pierce the potatoes and beets easily.

6. Remove the borscht from the heat and stir in the dill weed, salt, and pepper.

7. Divide the borscht into bowls. If you'd like, top each bowl with sour cream and dill weed and serve with rye bread and butter.

Norwegian Pytt i Panna Hash

Pytt i panna (PIHT ee paw-NUH) means "small pieces in a pan." Norwegians often make the dish to use up leftover vegetables, meat, and more.

Ingredients
(makes 4 servings)

- 7 tablespoons butter
- 1 onion, diced
- 6 potatoes, peeled and diced
- 2 carrots, peeled and diced
- 2 parsnips, peeled and diced
- ⅓ cup chicken stock
- 1½ pounds beef steak, cut into ½-inch (1.3-centimeter) cubes
- salt and pepper to taste
- 4 eggs
- fresh thyme (optional)

1. Melt 1 tablespoon butter in a frying pan over medium-high heat. Add the onion and cook until brown, about 10 minutes. Remove the onion from the pan and set it aside.

2. Melt 2 tablespoons butter in the pan. Add the potatoes, carrots, and parsnips. Cook for 10 minutes, stirring occasionally.

3. Add the chicken stock and cook until the liquid has boiled away. Remove the pan from heat.

4. Heat a large frying pan over high heat. Add the beef. Let the beef cook for about 2 minutes, flipping once, so it's browned but not fully cooked.

5. Add the potato mixture and onion to the beef. Stir together and cook until the beef is fully cooked, 3 to 5 minutes. Season with salt and pepper. Divide the hash onto plates.

6. Melt 1 tablespoon butter in a small pan over medium heat. Crack one egg in the pan and fry it until the white firms and the yolk starts to firm. Place the egg on top of a plate of hash. Repeat with the remaining eggs and butter. Serve each plate with a garnish of thyme if you'd like.

Enjoy!

Håper det smaker
(HO-peh deh SMA-keh)
means "enjoy
the food" in
Norwegian.

Mexican Lentil Soup

Lentil soup is popular in Mexico during Lent, a fasting period when some Christians do not eat meat.

Ingredients
(makes 4 servings)

- 1 tablespoon vegetable oil
- ½ onion, diced
- 2 carrots, peeled and diced
- 1 stalk celery, diced
- 1 clove garlic, minced
- 5 cups vegetable stock
- 1 tomato, diced
- 1 cup dry green or brown lentils, rinsed and dried
- 1 cube vegetable bouillon
- ½ teaspoon salt
- ½ teaspoon pepper
- ¼ teaspoon oregano
- ¼ cup chopped fresh cilantro
- fresh lime juice (optional)
- hot sauce (optional)

1. Heat the oil in a pot over medium-high heat. Add the onion, carrots, celery, and garlic. Cook until the vegetables soften, about 3 minutes.

2. Stir in the stock, tomato, lentils, bouillon, salt, pepper, and oregano. Bring the mixture to a boil and stir in the cilantro.

3. Reduce the heat to medium and cover the pot. Let the soup simmer for 18 to 20 minutes or until the lentils are soft. Stir the soup occasionally.

4. Serve the soup hot. For extra flavor, add a squeeze of lime juice and a few drops of hot sauce to each bowl.

Say It in Spanish

"Lentil soup" in Spanish is *sopa de lentejas* (SOH-pah day lehn-TAY-hahs).

Cuban
Beans and Rice

Cuban dishes have Spanish, Taino, Haitian, and Chinese influences. Many Cubans find beans and rice to be a comforting dish that reminds them of home.

Ingredients
(makes 6 servings)

- 6 slices bacon, chopped
- 1 onion, minced
- 6 cloves garlic, minced
- 1 green pepper, minced
- 1 teaspoon salt
- 2½ teaspoons chicken bouillon powder
- 2 bay leaves
- ½ teaspoon ground cumin
- 1 teaspoon oregano
- 1½ cups long grain white rice
- two 15.5-ounce cans black beans, with liquid
- 1 tablespoon red wine vinegar
- 1¾ cups water
- ½ cup chopped fresh cilantro (optional)

1. Heat a large frying pan over medium-high heat. Add the bacon and cook until it is browned, about 3 minutes on each side.

2. Add the onion, garlic, green pepper, and salt to the pan. Cook for 5 minutes or until the onion is translucent, stirring occasionally.

3. Add the bouillon, bay leaves, cumin, oregano, and rice to the pan. Stir until the rice is coated.

4. Stir in the beans and liquid, vinegar, and water.

5. Bring the mixture to a boil. Then reduce the heat to medium and cover the pan. Let the beans and rice simmer for 45 minutes. Do not remove the cover while the mixture cooks.

6. Remove the pan from heat and let it sit for 10 minutes.

7. Remove the cover and fluff the rice with a fork. Serve the dish with a sprinkle of cilantro if you'd like.

Arroz Congrí

Cuban beans and rice is sometimes called *arroz congrí* (ah-ROHS cohn-GREE).

Origins

Three-cup chicken was likely introduced to Taiwan by Chinese immigrants in the 1700s or 1800s. The dish is called *san bei ji* (sahn bay JEE) in Mandarin Chinese, Taiwan's official language.

Taiwanese Three-Cup Chicken

Three-cup chicken is named for the three liquids it contains: sesame oil, rice wine vinegar, and soy sauce. It is traditionally cooked and served in a clay pot.

Ingredients
(makes 4 servings)

- ¼ cup rice wine vinegar
- 3 tablespoons light soy sauce
- 1 tablespoon dark soy sauce
- 1½ tablespoons sugar
- ¼ cup sesame oil, plus extra
- 1-inch (2.5-cm) piece ginger, peeled and thinly sliced
- 10 cloves garlic, peeled
- 2 green onions, sliced
- 3 dried chili peppers
- 1 pound boneless, skinless chicken legs or thighs, cut into bite-size pieces
- 1 cup fresh Thai basil leaves, plus extra

1. Whisk the vinegar, soy sauces, and sugar together in a small bowl to make the sauce. Set it aside.

2. Heat the sesame oil in a pan over medium-high heat. Add the ginger and cook for 2 to 3 minutes or until it is browned.

3. Add the garlic and cook it for 1 minute. Stir in the green onion and chili peppers and cook for another minute.

4. Turn the heat to medium and add the chicken to the pan. Fry the chicken for 3 minutes, stirring constantly, until it is no longer pink.

5. Pour the sauce into the pan and stir to coat the chicken evenly. Turn the heat to medium high and keep stirring until the sauce starts to boil.

6. Reduce the heat to medium low. Simmer the chicken until the sauce thickens, stirring often.

7. Add the basil and simmer the dish for another 2 minutes, or until the basil softens. Garnish the dish with more basil leaves and a few drops of sesame oil.

Sierra Leonean Groundnut Soup

Many African countries have variations of groundnut (peanut) soup. In Sierra Leone, it is spicy and includes tomato. It is usually served with meat and rice.

Ingredients
(makes 6 servings)

- 6 chicken legs
- 3 teaspoons salt
- 2 teaspoons pepper
- 3 tablespoons olive oil
- 1 onion, chopped
- 1 jalapeno pepper, chopped
- 2 cloves garlic, minced
- 1 teaspoon fresh ginger, grated
- 1 tomato, chopped
- 1 tablespoon tomato paste
- 5 tablespoons smooth peanut butter
- 4 cups chicken stock
- 2 cups white rice, cooked

1. Pat the chicken legs dry with paper towels. Sprinkle the chicken with salt and pepper.

2. Heat the oil in a pan over medium-high heat. Carefully add the chicken legs and fry them until they are golden brown, about 4 minutes on each side. Set the chicken aside.

3. In the same pan, sauté the onion and jalapeno for 3 minutes or until soft. Stir in the garlic and ginger and cook for 1 minute. Then mix in the tomato and tomato paste.

4. Stir in the peanut butter and stock. Bring the soup to a low boil for 15 minutes, stirring occasionally. If the soup seems too thin, add more peanut butter to thicken it. If the soup is too thick, add more stock to thin it.

5. Continue to cook the soup for 15 to 30 minutes, or until oil bubbles to the top.

6. Add the chicken legs to the soup and cook for another 15 minutes. Serve one chicken leg and some rice with each soup serving.

Krio

Krio is the most-spoken language in Sierra Leone. It comes from formerly enslaved peoples of the U.S., West Indies, and Britain. "Rice" in Krio is *res* (REHS). "Groundnut" is *granat* (GRAH-naht).

Dinnertime

When the empanadas are ready, say "Es hora de cenar" (ehs OR-ah day SAY-nahr). This means "It's time for dinner" in Spanish, Argentina's official language.

Argentinean Empanadas

The Spanish likely brought empanadas (ehm-pah-NAH-dahs) to Argentina in the 1500s. While not traditional, using premade piecrusts makes this recipe quick and easy.

Ingredients
(makes 6 to 8 empanadas)

- 2 tablespoons vegetable oil
- 1 pound lean ground beef
- ¼ cup onion, diced
- ½ bell pepper, diced
- 1 teaspoon ground cumin
- 2 cloves garlic, minced
- ¼ teaspoon salt
- ¼ teaspoon pepper
- 1 teaspoon chili powder
- 1 package premade piecrusts (2 crusts total)
- 1 cup grated Mexican cheese
- 1 egg
- salsa (optional)
- guacamole (optional)

1. Preheat the oven to 375°F (190°C). Line a baking sheet with parchment paper and set it aside.

2. Make the filling. Heat the oil in a large frying pan over medium heat. Add the ground beef, onion, and bell pepper. Fry for 10 minutes or until the meat is browned and the vegetables are soft.

3. Mix in the cumin, garlic, salt, pepper, and chili powder. Cook for 2 to 3 minutes. Remove the pan from heat and set it aside.

4. Roll out the piecrusts on a floured surface. Use a cereal bowl to cut out three to four circles per crust.

5. Lay the crust circles on the baking sheet. Spoon 2 to 3 tablespoons of filling in the middle of each circle. Add 1 tablespoon of cheese.

6. Fold each circle in half over the filling. Press the edges together with a fork. Make sure the empanadas are evenly spaced on the baking sheet so they will cook evenly.

7. Whisk the egg in a small bowl. Brush some egg on top of each empanada.

8. Bake the empanadas for 12 to 15 minutes, or until the tops are golden brown. Serve with salsa and guacamole if you'd like.

Polish Haluski

This simple dish is a classic Polish comfort food. It is popular in Poland and other Eastern European countries for being simple, hearty, and inexpensive.

Ingredients
(makes 4 servings)

- 8 ounces egg noodles
- 6 tablespoons butter
- 12 ounces kielbasa, sliced
- 1 large onion, chopped
- 2 cloves garlic, minced
- 2 pounds green cabbage, chopped into bite-size pieces
- salt and pepper to taste

1. Cook and drain the noodles according to the package's directions. The noodles should be tender but still a bit firm and chewy. Set them aside.

2. Melt the butter in a large frying pan over medium-high heat. Add the kielbasa and onion. Cook until the kielbasa is crispy and the onion is soft, stirring often.

3. Reduce the heat to medium and add the garlic. Cook it for 1 minute, stirring constantly.

4. Add the cabbage to the pan and cook it until it is tender and soft, about 10 minutes.

5. Add the noodles to the pan and stir so the haluski is well mixed. Add salt and pepper to taste and serve the dish warm.

Haluski Meat

Kielbasa (keel-BAH-sah) is Polish sausage. Kielbasa and bacon are both often used in haluski (hah-LOOS-kee).

27

Yassa

The name *yassa* comes from the Portuguese word *assar* (AH-sahr), which means "to roast." The dish is called *yassa au poulet* (YAH-sah ow poo-LAY) in French, Senegal's official language.

Senegalese Chicken Yassa

Chicken yassa (YAH-sah) is a comfort food made in homes across Senegal. It is a unique blend of African, Portuguese, and French cuisines.

Ingredients
(makes 4 servings)

- 4 bone-in, skin-on chicken thighs
- 3 teaspoons salt
- 2 teaspoons pepper
- 3 medium onions, sliced
- 2 lemons, juiced
- 2 cloves garlic, minced
- 2 tablespoons Dijon mustard
- 3 tablespoons olive oil
- 3 tablespoons vegetable oil
- ½ habanero pepper, minced
- 1 cup water, plus extra
- ½ cup sliced green olives, plus extra for serving if desired
- 2 cups white rice, cooked

1. Pat the chicken dry with paper towels. Season the chicken with salt and pepper. Set it aside.

2. Place the onion in a bowl. Layer the chicken on top.

3. Whisk the lemon juice, garlic, mustard, olive oil, and habanero in a small bowl. This is the marinade.

4. Pour the marinade over the chicken and onion and toss to coat all pieces. Cover the bowl with plastic wrap and put it in the refrigerator for 3 to 12 hours.

5. Remove the chicken from the bowl. Put any onion pieces that were on the chicken back in the bowl.

6. Heat the vegetable oil in a large pan on medium-high heat. Fry the chicken in the pan until it is browned, about 4 minutes per side. Remove the chicken from the pan, leaving the drippings and oil.

7. Place the onion in the pan with ½ tablespoon marinade. Sauté the onion until slightly brown, about 10 minutes. Turn the heat to low and continue to brown the onion until caramelized, about 20 minutes.

8. Add the chicken, leftover marinade, and water to the pan. Cover and simmer for 10 minutes to finish cooking the chicken. Stir occasionally.

9. Add the olives to the pan. Let the dish simmer for 5 more minutes, or until the sauce is thick. Serve with rice and whole olives on the side.

English Cottage Pie

This dish dates to the 1700s. It was traditionally a way for people to use up leftover meat and veggies.

Ingredients
(makes 8 servings)

- 2 pounds ground beef
- 1 onion, diced
- 3 celery stalks, diced
- 3 carrots, peeled and diced
- 1 teaspoon salt
- 1 teaspoon pepper
- 5 cloves garlic, minced
- 4 tablespoons tomato paste
- 1 cup water
- ¼ cup all-purpose flour
- 3 cups beef stock
- 1 tablespoon chopped fresh thyme
- 1 tablespoon chopped fresh rosemary
- 1½ cups frozen peas
- 2 tablespoons Worcestershire sauce
- 4 cups cooked mashed potatoes
- ½ cup grated Parmesan cheese

1. Preheat the oven to 375°F (190°C).

2. Brown and break up the beef in a frying pan on medium heat. This should take 8 to 10 minutes.

3. Add the onion, celery, carrots, salt, and pepper. Cook the vegetables for 5 minutes or until they are soft. Add the garlic and cook for 2 minutes.

4. Stir in the tomato paste and cook for 3 minutes. Add the water and cook for 4 minutes or until the liquid is gone. Scrape brown bits off the bottom and sides of the pan with a wooden spoon.

5. Lower the heat to medium and stir in the flour. Cook for 1 to 2 minutes. Add the beef stock, thyme, rosemary, peas, and Worcestershire sauce and bring to a boil.

6. Turn the heat to medium low and simmer the mixture until the liquid is reduced by half. Pour the mixture into a large baking dish.

7. Spoon the mashed potatoes over the meat to completely cover it. Sprinkle ¼ cup cheese on top.

8. Place the dish on the oven's lower rack and bake for 20 to 25 minutes. Sprinkle the remaining cheese on top of the potatoes. Then move the dish to the top rack and turn the oven to broil. Broil for 2 to 4 minutes to lightly brown the potatoes. Let cool for 10 minutes before serving.

Cottage vs. Shepherd

Cottage pie is sometimes called shepherd's pie. But traditionally, cottage pie is made with beef while shepherd's pie is made with lamb.

Read More

Mara, Wil. *Food Around the World*. North Mankato, MN: Capstone, 2021.

Melian, Gaby. *Gaby's Latin American Kitchen: 70+ Kid-Tested and Kid-Approved Recipes for Young Chefs*. Boston: America's Test Kitchen, 2022.

Peterson, Tamara JM. *Colorful Foods in 15 Minutes or Less.* North Mankato, MN: Capstone, 2024.

Internet Sites

10 Delicious Kid-Friendly Foods of the World
lonelyplanet.com/articles/10-delicious-kid-friendly-foods-of-the-world

28 Different Potato Dishes from Around the World
thekidshouldseethis.com/post/28-ways-potato-dishes-around-the-world-video

Weeknight Dinner Around the World
nytimes.com/2019/09/24/dining/family-meals-around-the-world.html

About the Author

Chelsey Luciow is an artist and creator. She loves reading with kids and believes books are magical. Chelsey lives in Minneapolis with her wife, their son, and their dogs.